Sharing a book with your child is the perfect opportunity to cuddle and enjoy the reading experience together. Research has shown that reading with your child is one of the most important ways to prepare them for success as a reader. When you share books with each other, you help strengthen your child's reading and vocabulary skills as well as stimulate their curiosity, imagination and enthusiasm for reading.

In this book, Jake and his pirate crew bake Captain Hook a birthday cake. But what will happen when Hook tries to steal his own birthday cake? You can enhance the reading experience by talking to your child about their own experience of birthdays. What was their favourite birthday cake? If they baked a cake for a friend, what kind of cake would it be? Children find it easier to understand what they read when they can connect it with their own personal experiences.

Children learn in different ways and at different speeds, but they all require a supportive environment to nurture a lifelong love of books, reading and learning. The *Adventures in Reading* books are carefully levelled to present new challenges to developing readers. They are filled with familiar and fun characters from the wonderful world of Disney to make the learning experience comfortable, positive and enjoyable.

Enjoy your reading adventure together!

Scholastic Children's Books
Euston House,
24 Eversholt Street,
London NW1 1DB, UK

A division of Scholastic Ltd
London • New York • Toronto • Sydney • Auckland
Mexico City • New Delhi • Hong Kong

This book was first published in the United States in 2012 by Disney Press,
an imprint of Disney Book Group.
Published in Australia in 2014 by Scholastic Australia.
This edition published in the UK by Scholastic Ltd in 2015.

ISBN 978 1 4071 6297 3

Printed in Malaysia

2 4 6 8 10 9 7 5 3 1

www.scholastic.co.uk

LEVEL Pre-1

The Croc Takes the Cake

ADVENTURES IN READING

BY MELINDA LA ROSE

ILLUSTRATED BY ALAN BATSON

Today is Captain Hook's birthday.
'I want a birthday cake!' he yells.

Smee has made a fish cake.
'YUCK! That smells bad!'
yells Captain Hook.

'I want a *real* birthday cake,' says Captain Hook.

Cubby hears Captain Hook.
'I can make the best cake
for the captain,' he says.

'I will need all these things,' says Cubby. 'This will be a great cake!'

'I will help you,' says Izzy.
'So will I,' says Jake.

The cake is finished. Cubby and
Izzy take it to their ship.

Captain Hook sees the cake.
'I want that cake!' he says.

Captain Hook has a plan.
He steals the cake!

Hook falls into the Never Sea!
Oh no! The cake is in the water.

'Let's push the cake to Hook's ship,' says Jake. 'We can use the water cannons.'

Smee helps Hook back onto the ship.
'Here comes the cake!' he says.

'I can reach the cake!' says Smee.
'Hold onto my legs!'

He grabs at the cake. He misses the cake.

The cake is floating away.
'Crackers! Here comes
Tick-Tock the Croc,' says Skully.

Hook is scared. He jumps
into Smee's arms.

'Oh, coconuts!' says Cubby.
'The Croc will eat the cake.'

'I have an idea,' says Izzy.

Jake, Izzy and Cubby use pixie
dust. They fly to the cake.

They save the cake just in time!
'Here comes the cake,' says Smee.

'Happy birthday!' calls the crew.
'This cake is for you,' says Jake.

'Thank you!' says Hook.

Hook cuts his cake.
The pirates all take a slice.

'This is very yummy,' says Smee.
'And it doesn't taste like fish at all!'

'Now we are going back to Pirate Island,' says Izzy.

'Happy birthday!' the crew say.
They fly back to their ship.

'Well done, Cubby,' says Izzy.
'Hook really liked his birthday cake.'

'Oh, coconuts!' says Cubby.
'It felt good to do something nice!'

Today's Pirate Pledge

A good matey does nice things for other people.